BENEATH THE THORNS

Anaise Rose

BookLeaf
Publishing

India | USA | UK

Presentation by *BookLeaf Publishing*

Web: www.bookleafpub.com

E-mail: info@bookleafpub.com

ISBN: 9789358361179

First edition 2021

ACKNOWLEDGEMENT

For my mother up in heaven still shining her light. You have always been my saving grace, my rock, my wings. Love you always.

For my sister who truly holds the other half to my soul and makes me smile even in the darkest moments

For my dad that has helped me through the rough moments and allowed me to take my needed time to be under his wings and breathe

For the ones that are going through a rough patch and need to see themselves encapsulated in the words of these poems. For anyone that needs that extra push to keep looking forward and discover your own path. For the ones that are broken and need to dive into those feelings. This is for you.

PREFACE

I've never really aspired to be a writer of any kind. Growing up, I always preferred reading stories that were already created. I truly couldn't stay out of the bookstore or away from any book related event. The more dramatic and heart-wrenching the book was, the better in my opinion. I was one of the most bubbly and energetic kids around, obsessed with anything Disney and Nickelodeon themed but, I always craved the dark and depressing in relation to literature. I started to realize it stemmed from a fascination for the truth that exists in pain. It showed me what life is like when you aren't looking through rose-colored glasses. I knew life wasn't always a Disney World parade and I wanted to dive deeper into those stories. This is where my fascination with words truly began.

~ ~ ~ ~ ~ ~ ~ ~

I eventually got involved with more artistic tasks that involved helping my friend with spoken word/musical showcases and reaching out to my old dance organization to try and get involved with volunteering. In helping at my friend's showcases and seeing each performance, I realized how much I truly loved poetry and music. I always loved the lyrical beauty and simplicity of singer-songwriter music and the stories they tell. This music style speaks to me in a way that most others don't. It truly is my most curated playlist. Throughout my experience at these shows and teaching modern dance, I really started to delve deeper into my creativity. I sought for my class to not just simply be a dance class for my students but also a safe space for them to open up about their lives and connect through words. I chose this dance style mainly because it's where I connect most with my own body and mind. I chose music and choreography specifically for the girls to analyze and relate back to each other. Dancing became my visual poetry to tell a story and I encouraged my students to always tell theirs. Each word and rhythm had a connection and each week my students had the opportunity to dig deeper. We did this through creative worksheets, meditation, and spoken word podcasts. Additionally, I developed more of my writing style throughout the pandemic as I was able to more accurately capture my pain that was bottled up for so long.

~ ~ ~ ~ ~ ~ ~

Unfortunately, I lost my mother due to COVID and had a variety of health conditions arise and it really shattered my whole world. I struggled with different emotions that I couldn't completely grasp- pain, confusion, longing. It made me see struggle and pain in very different lights and these struggles inspired a lot of my writing. Poetry is what helps me find my center. I have always seen beauty in the words left unsaid and the ones you may not understand at first glance. But, that's the beauty of poetry. One poem creates a different story for each reader. I hope that my words do the same

"Paint me red or blue or any hue of you"

~Anaise Rose~

SUMMER

I love the way my cheeks blush red in the simmering glow of summer days and long steamy nights that inspire desire

While dancing raindrops fall off my torso in the summer rain, washing away the tears of yesterday

Cleansing the wounds of my transgressions and impurities in my soul

Wiping my spirit clean of all negativity

My chakras are centered as one

The sun brightening my skin, etching the trace of summer on my shoulders

Summer straps and flip flops leaving everlasting marks that fade with time

 Reminding me of hope & memories of sweet surrender

When my aura shined through the space in the trees that leads to the clouds

Oozing through the outstretched branches,
grasping to be let free and ascend far beyond
this land

To roam the sky and look down upon the world
and let out a breath, knowing that I have soared
above my fear & anguish

I smile at my newfound freedom with a tranquil
mind

I am free. I am me

CRIMSON PEAK

There's a peak that gleams bright in the distance

It guides me to follow its effervescent beauty

The mountain's crimson hue glowing just for me

The path won't be easy

The stones will pierce my flesh

The callouses on my feet reminders of the struggle and determination

But there is hope in the discovery

My skin is aflame with perseverance

Aglow with perspiration

But is my life whole? Or like a piece of Swiss? Pockets of holes resembling spaces that are unnaturally left empty

Wanting to be filled

Devoured

If I reach through to the other side, what will I
find?

I move past the pain

The bees that sting my flesh will not cause
trepidation

Not today

For that which stings is a reminder of life

Of honey coated dreams

Of affliction

Almost there, now

BREATHE

Strip away the skin & pieces of bone that
complete my body

Tie the strings that have unraveled my core

Put the puzzle pieces of my calamity back
together again

Follow the road map with twisted lines &
dead-end streets

Trace the glass with jagged edges to feel the
memory of my presence

Look through the windowpane, through the fog
& smoke, to see my untethered soul

Make me whole

Trust the vision of your soul

Call upon my name

Breathe me in

STARDUST

My threadbare soul lingers for a taste of truth

Head gazing up at the stars hoping for one
more moment of serenity

Before the merciless waves crash against the too
rocky shore

Revealing the harsh light of a new day

As I stare at my shadow in the waves which
reveals disco ball eyes glistening from tears not
too long ago washed away

And the specks of light trickle down my spine

Opening my soul

Revealing stardust in my vei

CONSTELLATIONS

There are specks of light that dance across rooftops.

They beckon you to notice & follow their magic within the hidden crevices of alleyways, where all is dark but not lost

Let the streetlamps illuminate your glow

Look up at the fire ablaze in the sky

The darkest corners of your mind scream at the solitude. They scream to be noticed

The sky is a blend of rainbow watercolors that perfectly blend the colors of my harmony

It ignites the fire of the constellations hidden in my soul & breathes new shimmering dreams into my reality

The sparks of fire flicker beneath my eyes as I blink away the pain and stare into the night,

past the deep abyss of wonder, with hope filled
tears

I cried with eyes that tried to hide the lies that
define me

I wait for fate to escape this crate of broken
pieces that bind me

ABYSS

I walk these empty streets with a kaleidoscope
of fragmented memories

Searching for a path to the mountain of souls

Desperate to find its peak

To sit on the edge of the cliff

Tossing rocks to and fro to see the depth of my
despair

Teetering with the fear of what's to come &
what does not yet exist

Balancing on tree branches, tempting fate

 If I fall, will I crumble into dust?

Another forgotten soul extending an arm for
their savior

Being let go into the abyss

DREAMS

Fresh sheets & gumdrop dreams

I sing to sleep in my serenity

Off to a place where pain is naught

And peace uplifts my chest and spirit

Where daisies whip against the morning air

Petals being carried by the wind

Remnants drifting across lakes once frozen over

Ascending into the clouds

Tranquil breaths and soul sparkling sighs
decorating my soul with a bouquet of hope as

I look up to the sky, and dare I say, release a
smile that emanates sparkles from my eyes

OBLIVION

Velvet wishes entrance all who notice the
pillowy smooth texture of deceit

The encapsulation of warmth on cold rainy
nights that allow you to cave into yourself

And, for a moment, allows you to forget the
lonely ache

The reality of what you long for

Tie dye smiles dripping watercolors down the
length of your frame

Until the reds, blues, and yellows become black
tar slipping through the cracked spine of your
too turned pages

Of the same story that's been told repeatedly
with no conclusion

Forever wondering the outcome

Forever wanting solace in knowing that there is
peace in the end

Forever needing the story to be rewritten and
retold with a brighter voice of hope and truth

With star speckled eyes and painted fingertips

Mixing the blues and yellows to become green

Not green with envy but with life

Uplifting nature trails leading to paths of
enlightenment and truth

Fingers grasping for the decadence of lilies and
lace that have dreams woven within its thread

Wonder begets hope as the thread untethers
and is pulled until there's nothing left

One last tiny string falling upon the broken
earth

Forgotten as it sinks into nothingness beneath
the cracks of the earth

Into oblivion

PARTY

Oh, how I miss those times

Those parties where laughs linger long past the start of the final toast

The kind where everyone's decadence outshines the ascending chandeliers

Where the jewelry hanging from too thin necks shines brighter than the gleaming china in the armoire

Standing in the spotlight, giving speeches we will soon forget

Dazzling smiles painted on faces long past the final goodbye

Pillow soft roses in every room

Silk pillowcases with petals on velvet sheets

Vanities with marble countertops filled with an array of jewels, revealing your vanity

Emeralds on the floor

Heels on broken skin revealing scars not long
ago healed

Bustier laced in place over breastbone

I am flourishing where I am

But it's time to go

I open the door, deep breath, and a smile, as I
return jaded kisses

WEEPING WILLOW

The weeping willows form an overcast path that
leads to an enclave of fenced off gardens

New patches of smooth damp earth exposed

It was there that I planted the seeds of violet
lilies and butternut squash colored daffodils

Petals outstretched with uplifting glory

Prideful in their beauty, their grace

Whispering songs soaked in stardust dreams

Singing "even as the seasons change and the
leaves fall, getting whipped away with time, you
are the unweathering branch with cherry
blossoms.

The reminder of strength and beauty amidst all
that is new.

Your strength will always shine through for you
are spreading your wings even when one is
broken"

DANCING SHADOWS

Campfire sunsets & vinyl tabletops

Collecting timber which tinders a flickering
spark

Record spinning, scratching with each climactic
trumpet's trill

Composing the breeze

As my dancing shadow twirls across the lake

Wandering aimlessly through my forsaken mind

Tilted head swirling with views of coastal
clouds and a pool or pearls

Floating far away, always moving, no end in
sight

Drifting into space

Smiling at the ignorance

TWILIGHT WOODS

Twilight embers & bourbon meadow dreams

Frosted branches and cranberry leaves

Vanilla skyline and evergreen trees

Velvet sunsets and marshy streams

These are the symbols of my serenity

Where doves fly high and coo with ease

Where feathers fall and brush my ashen skin, I crumble and repent my sins

For the Lord does know what's deep within

I cry and pray this time I'll win

I'll take the rock beneath my feet

And hold it 'til again we meet

Before I swim through jagged streams

To find the land of broken dreams

MEMORY

Oh good heavens my dear..

I'm not crying for you

Or me

I'm crying for the memory of what never was

The memory stripped away from my core that reduced me to futile space to help brighten your light

You know nothing but what you are and strive to be

I don't long for that which you never gave

Time which you never kept

Compassion which you never felt

It's okay my darling, the tide is coming

And will wash away all the lonely footprints on the shore

THE WIND

You never hear it calling when it comes

It swoops in and takes all that's whole with it

It sways to and fro, like a breathless winter morning

I want to go where it goes and see where it takes me. I hope one day it takes me to you

But for now, it serves as a reminder that there is something beyond, past the light above the mountain.

It reminds me that there's life beneath the rustling leaves, that there's beauty, that there's you

If I look past the clouds in the stillness, I can almost feel you. I feel you in everything I say and do

It makes me smile as it stirs up the wind within my heart that leads me to you.

I will always love you, through and through

EVERGREEN

There's a candle flickering in the wind

Flame holding on underneath the fiery sunset

Through my path of darkness, it illuminates my path through the tenuous journey

I am lost, but it finds me

I am breaking, but it guides me

Wolves howling at the full flower moon

As I wait to succumb to my fragile mind

Scraping tree trunks, ready for the fight

But this land is filled solely with eternal sunshine

With little bits of light peeking through the evergreens

With rubies and black onyx heartstones glimmering through the night's echo

Reminding you of your truth and the fire that
can't be extinguished

Tread on through the dimly lit valley, for on the
other side you will find peace and fields of roses
waiting to be plucked and taken on new
journeys

To be given to stargazing warriors to admire
their beauty

DANDELION

When we touch, I feel peace

Come, stay a while with me

Wrap me in your essence and smile at the flecks
in my eyes that you see through, that see you

Paint me in watercolors

Cover me in dandelions

Plant the seeds where you left me

Wish upon the stars that I'll be where you are

Fill up my space with your truth

As I pretend to know more than I do

Let me be close to you

Don't leave me in your rearview

I promise to hold the lock and key

For your gated community

BEYOND

One day far beyond the trees you'll see the unspeakable beauty. You'll see the rain, the sun, and the stars.

You'll feel the joy and peace of this earth beckoning you.

One brief moment of serenity and you'll see your reflection smiling back in the waves

BRUSHSTROKES

Fleeting moments. They are like brushstrokes
blending into one

Red and blue blend to become purple, those
colors soon forgotten. Time has erased them.

The bruises on my heart, the blood in my veins,
they are one in the same

They have disappeared with the night, just like
the distant memory of you

FIREFLY

Firefly eyes under watermelon skies

Hidden under canopy lights

Gleaming with wonder and joyful hope of a new
day that has been conquered

Clouds uncovering a harvest moon

Warmth spreading throughout my bones,
expanding my chest, stretching my limbs

Feeling the cracks of my bones breaking
through the ache

It signifies a life lived with struggle and desire

Always reaching for that which is out of grasp

Reaching for the constellations

Hoping to connect the stars and change my fate

DAWN

As I walk through the barren walls, I feel the empty shudder of the breeze passing through the doorways

Stirring up dust in its path that uncover old memories

Left untouched but not forgotten

Time frozen in place

But today, I change the clocks to the stroke of midnight

The promise of a new day

The rise of a new dawn

SUNSETS

There's a boat at the bay, docked, swaying to
and fro

I walk up to it and take both oars in my hand as
I stare into the river and the rainbow skies up
above

I know now that it's finally time to begin the
journey

 To brighter skies and aquamarine   seas…to
the land of saltwater tears & seashell shores

Footprints in the sand erased by the tumbling
tide A blank slate & chance to start anew

Toenails digging into the soft mound of the
sea…sand breaking apart in the wind's whisper

Ocean cream sunset casting a final glow on the
last night of broken memories

Making way for new light & beginnings

PURITY

There are spectacular uncertainties of truth

Of me and you

Of red and blue

Of all your hues

Of secret safe havens

With overflowing fountains of purity Make a
wish, my darling

For this moment in time will be a snapshot of
memories, held frozen by a Polaroid photograph

Edges crumpled and colors faded with use

But the feeling remains as do the rosy cheeks
and sweet pea smiles of careless youth

MISERY

With your lemonade lies, why cry, you darling
sly little wondrous being

It was you that caused this

 You that sought out this pain

 You that left the window open through the
storm

Blowing branches and rose thorns across your
doorstep

Leaving traces of your misery across the
creaking floorboards

WITHERING

There's one too many roses on your
mantlepiece

A cacophonous parade of charades

Like a pawn in a chess game

Never knowing where its piece will be moved

Moving forward to reach the road less travelled,
but not knowing when it will meet its demise

An existential end on a broken path

Looking forward to looking back on these
distant memories

Losing track of love as you creep further into
the distance

RISE ABOVE

You threw stones from my garden at my windows

And left holes in the spaces that used to be whole

My petals have fallen, leaving me empty, unseen, unrefined

But with darkness comes new light

New beauty & new life

I am blooming through the pain and shame

Sprouting through the airy morning

Creating new roots

Moving past you into the big beyond

I have superseded you and the hurt

The thorns have been plucked from the roses you gave and my pierced skin drips, leaving a path of pain behind as a reminder

But I moved past this land

You can follow until you reach the fork in the road that leads away from you

Into freedom and sunshine

As I frolic through the field of daisies

Feeling the dew of the petals under my fingertips

Smelling the fresh rain that has washed away any semblance of pain in this land

I am here

ECLIPSE

The moon's beauty is deep & dark & endless

It's the polar opposite of the sun, but yet, its
beauty shines brighter

Through the mysterious fog in the woods

Past the howling of the wolves

On a cold dark night by the lake

I felt you there, beckoning me

———————

I hope, one day, I find you

I hope, one day, you instill peace within my
bones

Hope within my soul

Breath within my lungs

Life within the reservoirs of the chambers of my
heart

I hope, one day, that the smile reaches my eyes

The laughter reaches my chest

And the fire ignites my voice

____

But that's just it

Don't you see the collateral beauty?

Hope is but a figment of time

The desire in your heart burns brighter than
the sun

Don't let it consume you, but see where it takes
you

Follow the stars

Follow the light of the moon

Follow the rustling of the leaves

Follow the light beneath the hollows of your
eyes

Follow peace

And it is there, that you will find me

PRISM

I aspire to be like the wind

Light and airy.. floating and weightless

I dream to be like the stars

Gleaming beauty that shines brighter in the
darkest moments

Where everything that's broken dissipates in
the glow of midnight

The shattered glass that was etched into the
soles of my bare feet have come together to
form a prism of watercolors

Dripping off the paint brush, forming a swirl of
beauty & illusion

A burst of color and life

From the depths of my pain, I found hope,
grace, wonder, strength

I found me

I found truth

GLOW

There is a place beyond the pines filled with
magical creatures

It tells stories of the paths life have taken them

It whispers melodies of safe havens that exist in
our own hearts if we look closely enough

There you will find the holes dug deep in the
earth to uncover the new life that sprouts light
within her eyes, those eyes that sparkle brighter
when she smiles and takes in new breath

The dewy sunshine drips from her lips as she
caresses the new morning and bathes in the
sunlight

The sun's rays glinting off the freckles of her
skin

It is in this bright glow that you see the
incandescent beauty of the blood running
through her veins

The violet orchids bloom from the bushes,
indicating spring blooming to life

She caresses them like a soft kiss

Taking in the honeydew scent of peace

She places them against her breastbone and
remembers the feeling of grasping for a
lingering lost love

The fragility of something being so delicately
profound that it screams for you to notice its
presence

Its whimsical aura of being

Of truth

Of light

FLAMES

There is a room at the end of the hall that
houses things left untouched by flames

Flames that have burnt all that's pure

Leaving ash in the floor cracks and crevices of
your memories

Dropping stones in the fountain, making wishes
that won't come true

Leaving a path of trailing daisies with no petals
that lead to rose bushes with only thorns

Where you lead, I follow

Down the road of despair and the path of
disappointments

WATERCOLOR

Paint me with the colors of stardust &
daydreams

Moon shadows & honeysuckle

Paint me black & blue

Or any hue of you

Let the strokes drip from the canvas into the
cracks of the floor that creak with the faint
footsteps that have walked across my heart

Leave your footprints for me to follow through
the forest

When it's dark & cold and no light illuminates
my path

I will follow the echoes of my heart to lead me
back to you